Getting Along
WITH
YOUR FAMILY

A 4-week course to help senior highers discover God's plan for families

by Lois Keffer

Group
Loveland, Colorado

Getting Along With Your Family
Copyright © 1992 Group Publishing, Inc.

First Printing

Credits
Edited by Stephen Parolini
Cover designed by Diane Whisner
Illustrations by Raymond Medici
Cover photo by Brenda Rundback and David Priest

ISBN 1-55945-233-1
Printed in the United States of America

CONTENTS

GETTING ALONG WITH YOUR FAMILY

Families are an endangered species.

In our highly mobile, economically pressured society, the image of a securely planted, two-parent family complete with uncles, aunts, cousins and grandparents has faded into nostalgic oblivion. One in two marriages is destined for divorce. Many authorities point to father absence as the root problem behind gangs and urban violence. Media models and MTV encourage kids to grab for surface relationships, then to let go when things get sticky.

Even the lucky kids who live in committed, two-parent families are likely to get precious little of their parents' time and attention. Job and school demands and social schedules keep kids and parents on the run. "Quality family time" has become a wistful, if not impossible, dream.

This course will help senior highers understand God's purpose for families. Kids will explore why families are important and what scripture teaches about family priorities. They'll discover family roles and how to work at making their family relationships the best they can be. They'll discuss sources of family conflict and practice positive ways to approach conflict resolution.

Families are worth preserving—and it's going to be a battle. The very first family God created suffered conflict and tragedy. But families are still God's best plan for us. Today's

The American Family Status

Check out these stats on families in the United States today:

- 88 percent of adults believe it's harder to be a parent today than it used to be.
- 87 percent of adults say parents today have a hard time making ends meet.
- 81 percent of adults say parents today don't spend enough time with their kids.
- 76 percent of adults say parents often don't know where their children are or what they're doing.
- 25 percent of American kids live with just one parent.

kids need all the relational skills, wisdom and biblical understanding we can give them to survive family turbulence now and build strong families in the future.

By the end of this course, your students will
- discover positive and negative effects their attitudes and actions can have on their families,
- experience the pressures parents face,
- make a commitment to strengthen their family relationships,
- plan ways to defuse family conflicts and
- compare their present families to how they envision their future families.

COURSE OBJECTIVES

HOW TO USE THIS COURSE

ACTIVE LEARNING

Think back on an important lesson you've learned in life. Did you learn it from reading about it? from hearing about it? from something you experienced? Chances are, the most important lessons you've learned came from something you experienced. That's what active learning is—learning by doing. And active learning is a key element in Group's Active Bible Curriculum™.

Active learning leads students in doing things that help them understand important principles, messages and ideas. It's a discovery process that helps kids internalize what they learn.

Each lesson section in Group's Active Bible Curriculum plays an important part in active learning:

The **Opener** involves kids in the topic in fun and unusual ways.

The **Action and Reflection** includes an experience designed to evoke specific feelings in the students. This section also processes those feelings through "How did you feel?" questions and applies the message to situations kids face.

The **Bible Application** actively connects the topic with the Bible. It helps kids see how the Bible is relevant to the situations they face.

The **Commitment** helps students internalize the Bible's message and commit to making changes in their lives.

The **Closing** funnels the lesson's message into a time of creative reflection and prayer.

When you put all the sections together, you get a lesson that's fun to teach. And kids get messages they'll remember.

BEFORE THE 4-WEEK SESSION

● Read the Introduction, the Course Objectives and This Course at a Glance.

● Decide how you'll publicize the course using the clip art on the Publicity Page (p. 9). Prepare fliers, newsletter articles and posters as needed.

● Look at the Bonus Ideas (p. 46) and decide which ones you'll use.

● Read the opening statements, Objectives and Bible Basis for the lesson. The Bible Basis shows how specific passages relate to senior highers today.

● Choose which Opener and Closing options to use. Each is appropriate for a different kind of group.

● Gather necessary supplies from This Lesson at a Glance.

● Read each section of the lesson. Adjust where necessary for your class size and meeting room.

BEFORE EACH LESSON

● The approximate minutes listed give you an idea of how long each activity will take. Each lesson is designed to take 35 to 60 minutes. Shorten or lengthen activities as needed to fit your group.

● If you see you're going to have extra time, do an activity or two from the "If You Still Have Time . . ." box or from the Bonus Ideas (p. 46).

● Dive into the activities with the kids. Don't be a spectator. The lesson will be more successful and rewarding to both you and your students.

● Though some kids may at first think certain activities are "silly," they'll enjoy them, and they'll remember the messages from these activities long after the lesson is over. As one Active Bible Curriculum user has said, "I can ask the kids questions about a lesson I did three weeks ago, and they actually remember what I taught!" And that's the whole idea of teaching . . . isn't it?

Have fun with the activities you lead. Remember, it is Jesus who encourages us to become "like little children." Besides, how often do your kids get *permission* to express their childlike qualities?

HELPFUL HINTS

● The answers given after discussion questions are responses your students *might* give. They aren't the only answers or the "right" answers. If needed, use them to spark discussion. Kids won't always say what you wish they'd say. That's why some of the responses given are negative or controversial. If someone responds negatively, don't be shocked. Accept the person, and use the opportunity to explore other angles of the issue.

THIS COURSE AT A GLANCE

Before you dive into the lessons, familiarize yourself with each lesson aim. Then read the scripture passages.
● Study them as a background to the lessons.
● Use them as a basis for your personal devotions.
● Think about how they relate to kids' circumstances today.

LESSON 1: WHO NEEDS FAMILIES?

Lesson Aim: To help senior highers accept responsibility for helping create a healthy family environment.
Bible Basis: Genesis 2:18-24 and Deuteronomy 6:1-9.

LESSON 2: FAMILY ROLES AND HOW THEY'RE PLAYED

Lesson Aim: To help senior highers understand typical family roles and explore God's standards for family relationships.
Bible Basis: Luke 15:11-32 and Romans 12:4-10.

LESSON 3: THE NUCLEAR FAMILY

Lesson Aim: To help senior highers learn how to resolve conflict in positive, Christlike ways.
Bible Basis: Matthew 18:15-16 and Luke 10:38-42.

LESSON 4: YOUR FUTURE FAMILY

Lesson Aim: To help senior highers think through their goals and dreams for their future families.
Bible Basis: Jeremiah 29:11-13 and Matthew 7:24-27.

PUBLICITY PAGE

Grab your senior highers' attention! Photocopy this page, and then cut out and paste the clip art of your choice in your church bulletin or newsletter to advertise this course on families. Or photocopy and use the ready-made flier as a bulletin insert. Permission to photocopy this clip art is granted for local church use.

Splash the clip art on posters, fliers or even postcards! Just add the vital details: the date and time the course begins and where you'll meet.

It's that simple.

Getting Along
WITH YOUR FAMILY

GETTING ALONG
WITH YOUR
FAMILY

A 4-week high school course to help teenagers build positive relationships in their families

Come to _____

On _____

At _____
_____

Come discover how to be the best family member you can be!

WHO NEEDS FAMILIES?

A house with teenagers under the roof is seldom a tranquil place. While kids assert their growing need for independence, parents do their best to establish and keep safe boundaries. When home life seems to become a never-ending set of hassles, kids may begin to think, "Who needs families, anyway?"

This lesson will help your teenagers recognize that even far-from-perfect families meet important needs in their lives and that their own habits and attitudes have a major impact on the quality of family life.

To help senior highers accept responsibility for helping create a healthy family environment.

LESSON AIM

OBJECTIVES

Students will
- discover the positive and negative effects their attitudes and actions can have on their families,
- explore God's reasons for placing them in families,
- compare personal and family traits and
- define how to make a positive impact on their family environments.

Look up the following scriptures. Then read the background paragraphs to see how the passages relate to your senior highers.

In **Genesis 2:18-24**, God states that it isn't good for people to be alone, even in a perfect paradise. We're created with a basic need for fellowship and intimacy, both with God and with fellow humans.

The very first family on earth experienced devastating

BIBLE BASIS
GENESIS 2:18-24
DEUTERONOMY 6:1-9

problems and grief, but their tragedy didn't cause God to alter his plan for families. Teenagers need to see that, while there's no such thing as a perfect family, God put us in families so our basic needs can be met, and he expects us to work at our family relationships.

In **Deuteronomy 6:1-9**, God defines a primary function of families: to teach children to live in God's love and in obedience to God's commands.

Each generation of Christians lives only a few decades. Families hold the crucial responsibility of passing on God's truth so that it survives from one generation to the next.

Children who learn love and discipline from wise earthly fathers find it easy to accept love and guidance from their heavenly Father. Teenagers who are eager to shed parental discipline will make the step to independence successfully if they rely on the faith and obedience they learned to accept in their early years.

THIS LESSON AT A GLANCE

Section	Minutes	What Students Will Do	Supplies
Opener (Option 1)	5 to 10	**Pulling Away**—Tie themselves together and pull in opposite directions.	5-foot lengths of rope
(Option 2)		**Nobody's Perfect**—Compare imperfect circles to families.	Pencils, paper
Action and Reflection	10 to 15	**No Winners**—Experience having someone disrupt a game so no one can win.	Dominoes
Bible Application	15 to 20	**God's Best Plan**—Discover why God put them in families.	Tape, newsprint, marker, Bibles
Commitment	5 to 10	**Family Types**—Identify their family types and choose one thing they'd like to improve.	"What's Your Family Type?" handouts (p. 19), pencils, envelopes
Closing (Option 1)	up to 5	**Personal Atmosphere**—Compare the scent of perfume to the atmosphere they create.	Cologne, perfume
(Option 2)		**Family Prayers**—Pray for each other's families.	

...ive each

...ur family," stand

...ng the

...er.

...ng in a ...to-

gether, it might be more comfortable to be on your own.)

Have all the family groups move to the center of the room. Say: **Find out which person in your group got up the earliest this morning. That person will be the teenager. Turn your family so the teenager is facing one of the corners of the room. When I say "go," the teenager will pull your family toward the corner he or she is facing. The rest of you will do your best to stay right where you are. Ready? Go!**

Allow the struggle to go on for a minute or two. Then call time and ask the "teenagers":

● **How did it feel to try to pull in a different direction from the rest of your family?** (Frustrating; exhausting.)

Ask the rest of the "family" members:

● **How did it feel to hold your family in place?** (Pretty easy since there were more of us; I got tired of trying.)

● **How is this like what sometimes happens in your real families?** (It feels like they're always holding me back; I don't get to do what I like to do.)

Have families untie the ropes that are holding them together.

Say: **Now everybody stretch and shake out.**

Ask:

● **How is this like what a lot of kids would like to do?** (We want to shake free of our parents and stand on our own.)

Say: **As you approach the end of high school, your family naturally begins to feel more and more restrictive. Sometimes you'd probably like to shake free of parental authority and strike out on your own. Sometimes it may feel like freedom and independence are light-years away. That's why it's important for us to take a look at how families work and why God put us in families in the first place.**

☐ OPTION 2: NOBODY'S PERFECT

Give each student a pencil and a sheet of paper. Have kids form groups of no more than four.

Say: **The group you're in now will be your "family" for this entire lesson. You have 60 seconds to decide as a family how to finish this statement: "A family is..." Go!**

After a minute call time and ask each family to share its response.

Then say: **Please sit on the floor in your family group with your back to your family members. Draw a quarter of a circle on your paper. If there are three in your family, draw a third of a circle. Draw your portion very carefully so that when you put it together with the portions your family members draw, you'll have a complete circle. No fair looking at each other's papers. Go!**

After about 30 seconds, call time and have families put their papers together. Invite groups to get up and look at how other families' circles came out.

Ask:

● **Why did these circles come out so badly?** (Because we couldn't see what our other family members were doing; because nobody can draw a perfect circle.)

● **How are these imperfect circles like your real-life families?** (Nobody has a perfect family; all our families are made out of imperfect people.)

Say: **Living with imperfect people in an imperfect family can be quite a strain.** *(Pick up one family's papers and crumple them.)* **Sometimes you may even feel like calling it quits. But God is the one who started families in the first place, and he did it for some pretty good reasons. Today we're going to discover what some of those reasons are and think about how we can each work to make our families a little bit better.**

ACTION AND REFLECTION
(10 to 15 minutes)

NO WINNERS

Ask each family to send you one representative. Take the representatives aside or outside the room and say: **I'm going to give each of you a set of dominoes. Take them to your family and explain that you're supposed to work together to build a tower. The family that builds the highest tower in three minutes wins. I'll cough just before the three minutes are up. That's your secret signal to say something like, "I don't like this dumb tower," and knock it over. Don't let on that this is a planned demolition.**

Have the representatives return to their families with the dominoes. Give the signal for the beginning of the three-minute building period. Emphasize that there's enough time to do a careful job. As you see that one of the towers is about to be completed, give the coughing signal.

Look at the ruined towers with mock disbelief and say: **Whoa—what happened here? You guys were going great.**

Now it looks like we won't have any winners.

As kids begin to accuse you of setting up the activity for failure, say: **You all know what happened here. I set up this activity to self-destruct.**

Ask:

● **How did you feel when your representative suddenly destroyed your tower?** (I thought, "Oh, great!"; I figured something like this would happen.)

● **How is this self-destruction like what sometimes happens in families?** (It only takes one person's negative attitude to ruin things for everyone else.)

Say: **One of the most remarkable things about families is that we often save our worst behavior for those we love the most. Here's some simple proof. Turn to the people in your family group and tell them about two compliments you've given recently to people in your real-life family.**

Allow a few moments for sharing. Then say: **Now tell the people in your group about two negative comments you've made recently to people in your real-life family.**

After a few more moments, call everyone together and ask:

● **Which was easier to think of—compliments you'd given or negative comments?**

If most kids don't reply that negative comments came to mind more easily, they're probably putting you on!

Ask:

● **Why do you think we tend to save our worst behavior for those who are closest to us?** (We know they'll love us no matter how we behave; dumping is a two-way street—they do it to us, so we do it to them.)

● **How do you think the atmosphere in your family would change if everyone made an attempt to be positive and affirming?** (That's an impossible dream; if everyone really worked at it, it might make a big difference.)

Say: **We don't want to turn our homes into a place where nobody wins. One person's positive effort can make a big difference in how a family feels. And we know that our families are worth that kind of effort because the Bible places high value on families. Let's take a few minutes to discover how and why families got started and what God expects from families today.**

GOD'S BEST PLAN

Tape a large sheet of newsprint onto the wall. With a marker, write at the top of the newsprint, "Who Needs Families?" Then say: **Let's make a list of things our families supply for us. We'll go around the room, and each family can add one thing at a time to the list.**

Have families take turns adding to the list until everyone is out of ideas. Then say: **We've made a pretty significant list of things we depend on our families to provide for us. Now let's choose the top five items on the list. Of all**

BIBLE APPLICATION
(15 to 20 minutes)

these things listed here, which would you least want to do without?

Put a star by each of the items kids suggest. Then say: **Let's go to the Bible to discover God's priorities for families.**

Have a volunteer read aloud Genesis 2:18-24. Then ask:

● **From God's perspective, what important human needs does a family meet?** (The need for companionship, help and a sense of belonging.) Jot down kids' responses in a second list.

Have another volunteer read Deuteronomy 6:1-9 aloud. Again ask:

● **From God's perspective, what important human needs does a family meet?** (The need to learn about God's love and God's rules; the need to learn discipline and obedience; the need to live in a peaceful, prosperous community.)

After you've listed kids' responses, say: **Let's compare our two lists. How closely does our list of needs compare to the needs we found in the two Bible passages?** (They're pretty close; we were way off.)

Say: **With these lists in mind, let's take a look at some different types of families and see how our families shape who we become.**

COMMITMENT
(5 to 10 minutes)

FAMILY TYPES

Give each student a "What's Your Family Type?" handout (p. 19) and a pencil.

Say: **This handout is for your personal use only—no one else will see it. Take a couple of minutes to evaluate where your family fits on the scale in each of the categories. After you've carefully rated your family, go back and rate yourself personally in each category.**

Chances are, you'll have kids from single-parent or blended families in your group. These kids may carry a lot of bitterness or erroneously blame themselves for their circumstances. Make it a point to see that these kids don't see themselves as second-class citizens. Emphasize the fact that no family is perfect and that we can't take responsibility for other people's actions.

Call time after about three minutes and ask:

● **How closely did your personal ratings match the ratings you gave your family?** (Pretty close; not close at all.)

Say: **There's no doubt that our families have a lot to do with who we become. But you individually can also have a big influence on what your family is like. Turn your papers over and write, "One thing I'd like to improve about my family is . . . " I'll give you a moment to finish that sentence.**

Pause, then say: **Okay, now write, "One step I can take to make that improvement is . . . " But before you finish** that sentence, let me remind you that you can't change other people; you can only change your behavior and your responses. So think carefully about something you can do to bring about positive change. Don't try to take responsibility for anyone else's behavior. Now finish the sentence by stating a reasonable goal—something you can do this week.

As kids are writing, distribute envelopes. Have kids write their names on their envelopes and seal their handouts inside. Collect the envelopes and say: **I'm going to tuck these away in a safe place and give them back to you when we get to Lesson 4.**

Table Talk

The Table Talk activity in this course helps senior highers talk with their parents about family relationships.

If you choose to use the Table Talk activity, this is a good time to show students the "Table Talk" handout (p. 20). Ask them to spend time with their parents completing it.

Before kids leave, give them each the "Table Talk" handout to take home, or tell them you'll be sending it to their parents. Tell kids to be prepared to report next week on their experiences with the handout.

Or use the Table Talk idea found in the Bonus Ideas (p. 47) for a meeting based on the handout.

OPTION 1: PERSONAL ATMOSPHERE

Have kids re-form their family groups.

Say: **Choose a representative from your family for a highly privileged task.**

Take the representatives out of the room and spray each of them with cologne or perfume. If possible, use a masculine scent for the guys and a feminine fragrance for the girls.

Bring the representatives back into the room and say: **Please stand in a circle around your family representative and hold hands.**

Ask:

● **What do you notice about your representative?** (He [or she] smells good.)

● **How is the atmosphere your perfumed person creates like the personal atmosphere your moods and attitudes create within your family?** (When I'm tense and angry that tension spreads through the whole family; when I'm really up about something it cheers up everyone else.)

Have the perfumed representatives join their circles.

Say: **Beginning with your privileged perfumed person, tell the person on your left one positive thing he or she brings to his or her family. For example, you might say, "You bring your family a sense of humor" or "You bring a creative imagination to your family."**

Close with a brief prayer for the families represented in

CLOSING
(up to 5 minutes)

your group. As kids leave, hit them with a shot of fragrance and encourage them to bring a positive atmosphere to their families this week.

☐ OPTION 2: FAMILY PRAYERS

Have kids sit together in their family groups.

Say: **Tell your group one way it can pray for your real-life family this week. Then, beginning with the person who has the cleanest shoes, go around your circle and pray a sentence prayer for the family of the person on your left.**

If You Still Have Time . . .

Hysterical Moments—Invite kids to share classic, funny family stories. Kick off the laughs with a story of your own.

Tail Lites—Distribute paper and markers. Have kids anonymously create humorous bumper stickers for their family cars. Collect the creations and have kids guess who made which.

WHAT'S YOUR Family TYPE?

Put a star on the scale where your family fits. Neither side of
the scale is good or bad—they just reflect different styles.

	1	2	3	4	5	
homebodies						adventurous
thrifty	1	2	3	4	5	spenders
serious	1	2	3	4	5	fun-loving
outgoing	1	2	3	4	5	laid-back
argumentative	1	2	3	4	5	agreeable
relaxed	1	2	3	4	5	high-geared
sophisticated	1	2	3	4	5	straightforward

Now go through the chart again and put a check by
where you personally fit in each category.

Table Talk

To the Parent: We're involved in a senior high course at church called *Getting Along With Your Family*. Your teenager is learning about how families operate and what God expects of family members. We'd like you and your teenager to spend some time discussing this important topic. Use this "Table Talk" page to help you do that.

Parent

● What's one thing you really admire about your teenager?

● How would you feel about being a teenager in today's world?

● What's one thing your teenager does that drives you up the wall? What can you do to resolve that issue?

Senior higher

● Do you ever feel concern or worry about your parent? Explain.

● What's one thing your parent did for you that sticks out in your mind as something you really appreciated and will never forget?

● What's one thing you wish your parent would quit bugging you about? What can you do to resolve that issue?

Parent and senior higher

Parent: On a separate sheet of paper list five things you think your teenager wants from you. Also list five things you really want from your teenager.

Teenager: On a separate sheet of paper list five things you think your parent wants from you. Also list five things you really want from your parent.

Compare your lists to see if you're on the same wavelength. Work through your lists and discuss specific ways you can meet each other's needs and expectations.

Together read aloud Ephesians 6:1-4.

● How do the needs and expectations you listed reflect or conflict with the principles stated in this passage?

FAMILY ROLES AND HOW THEY'RE PLAYED

It's almost magical how families develop roles and how consistently the players stick with their "assigned" characters. Some of your students may love the clown role; others play the strong leader, the princess or the go-between. These and many other roles start at home and often carry over into school, church and social situations.

This lesson helps kids take a close look at the roles they play in their families and how those roles affect their relationship to God and to each other.

To help senior highers understand typical family roles and explore God's standards for family relationships.

LESSON AIM

OBJECTIVES

Students will
- analyze the "ripple effect" in family behavior,
- experience the pressures parents face,
- discover how birth order may affect their relationships,
- relate to the feelings of both sons in the story of the prodigal son and
- make a commitment to strengthen their family relationships.

BIBLE BASIS
LUKE 15:11-32
ROMANS 12:4-10

Look up the following scriptures. Then read the background paragraphs to see how the passages relate to your senior highers.

In **Luke 15:11-32**, Jesus recounts the parable of the prodigal son.

In this familiar story the two brothers follow classic birth order patterns. The first-born son is straight-arrow—disciplined, hard-working and eager to please the father. The last-born is a misfit who isn't even slightly interested in trying to live up to his brother's shining example.

The father is a truly interesting character. He didn't balk at dividing the estate prematurely. He let the younger son learn the hard way—from real-life mistakes. And when the prodigal returned, the father literally welcomed him with open arms and graciously restored him to his previous status in the family.

Our God is like the forgiving father in the story. One spurt of rebellion doesn't spell the end of the relationship. Grace intervenes where judgment would condemn and cut off. What great news for high schoolers! As they struggle with the process of relating to parents and siblings and gaining independence, there may be some side trips in the wrong direction. But grace is greater than sin, and reconciliation is always an option.

Romans 12:4-10 deals with spiritual gifts and brotherly love—both important factors in family living.

Churches and families can be destroyed by jealousy and competition. The fact is, every individual is gifted in one way or another, so there's no need for guarding territory and putting each other down.

Teenagers are so preoccupied with themselves that they give little thought to how their activities impact other family members. Kids need to understand that they don't endanger their own status by honoring others above themselves. Thinking of others is a lot to ask of teenagers, but it's one of the keys to establishing sound relationships in their present and future families.

Section	Minutes	What Students Will Do	Supplies
Opener (Option 1)	5 to 10	**The Big Ripple**—Experience falling over when one person is pushed.	
(Option 2)		**Impossible Task**—Complete a task that depends on each member of a trio performing a role.	Blindfolds, masking tape, markers, paper
Action and Reflection	10 to 15	**Rat Race**—Watch as a "parent" participates in a difficult race.	Masking tape, hymnals, chocolate kisses, 3×5 cards, newsprint, marker
Bible Application	15 to 20	**What's Your Role?**—Compare the roles in the story of the prodigal son to family roles they play today.	Posterboard, marker, Bibles
Commitment	5 to 10	**Roles Reconsidered**—Evaluate responses to family situations.	"Roles Reconsidered" handout (p. 29), scissors, Bibles
Closing (Option 1)	up to 5	**Family Assets**—Affirm each other's value to their families.	Paper plates, markers
(Option 2)		**Surprised!**—Tell partners one surprising thing they learned about themselves.	

The Lesson

OPTION 1: THE BIG RIPPLE

Have kids line up elbow to elbow facing you. Make sure kids are standing close together.

Say: **Today we're going to be talking about the different roles people play in their families. Let's start off with me being the strong leader.** (Flex your muscles a bit or strike a power pose.) **Watch me carefully and do exactly as I do.**

Give directions in this sequence:

● **Raise one arm straight toward the ceiling and hold it there.**

● **Go down on one knee.**

● **Still on one knee, tuck your other arm behind your back.**

● **Drop your head forward so your chin is nearly resting on your chest.**

At this point your students will be in a very vulnerable position balance-wise, and they won't be able to see you very well. Step over to the first person in line and give him or her a little push. The whole row will fall over like dominoes. This is a safe move since kids are already close to the ground.

OPENER
(5 to 10 minutes)

As kids are picking themselves up, say: **This is what I call the "ripple effect." One little move I made suddenly had disastrous results for the rest of the group.**

Ask:

● **How is this like what happens in families?** (One person's actions can throw everyone else off; everyone has to live with the effects of what everyone else does.)

Say: **Sixteenth-century poet John Donne wrote the famous line, "No man is an island." Most of us inhabit a house or apartment with at least one other person. Today we're going to look at the roles we play in our families and how those roles can affect us for the rest of our lives.**

☐ OPTION 2: IMPOSSIBLE TASK

Form trios.

Say: **In each trio one person can't see, one person can't speak and the third person can't move.** Have trio members choose their roles. Hand out blindfolds for eyes and masking tape for mouths and ankles. When trios have appropriately disabled themselves, say: **Here's your task: Find out the Social Security number of each person in your trio. Write the numbers on a sheet of paper taped to the back of a member of your trio. The markers, tape and paper are in the** (furnace room or other inconvenient location). **You've got five minutes. Go!**

Enjoy watching the strategy as trios struggle to complete their task. Call time after five minutes and applaud kids' efforts whether they succeeded in their task or not.

Ask:

● **What was the most challenging thing about this activity?** (Deciding how to tackle it; working together when each member was only partially functional.)

● **How was this like working together as a family?** (Each person has strengths and weaknesses; you have to work together to get things done.)

Say: **In families, just as in our trios, each member needs to play his or her role. What one person does or doesn't do affects everyone. Today we're going to take a closer look at family roles and how our families work together.**

Table Talk Follow-Up

If you sent the "Table Talk" handout (p. 20) to parents last week, discuss students' reactions to the activity. Ask volunteers to share what they learned from the discussion with their parents.

RAT RACE

Mark a starting line with masking tape about 3 feet from one end of the room. Form teams of four and have each team choose a "parent." Give each team a hymnal and three chocolate kisses. Line up the teams behind the starting line. Place a chair at the other end of the room opposite each team.

Say: **This is a rat race, and here's how it goes. Each team will balance its hymnal on the head of its parent. The parent will hold the chocolate kisses and walk to the other end of the room, circle the chair and come back to the team. Still balancing the book, the parent will unwrap the chocolate kisses, place one kiss in the mouth of each team member, then circle the chair again and return to the team. Okay, parents, heads up! Teams, balance your books.**

When a book is balanced on each parent's head, say "go!" Encourage the teams to cheer their parents on. Each time a parent drops a book, have him or her stop and replace the book before starting again.

At the end of the race, give all the parents a round of applause. Ask the kids who sat on the sidelines:

● **How did it feel watching your parent struggle to finish the race?** (I felt sorry for our group's parent; I wished I could've helped.)

Ask the parents:

● **How did it feel balancing the book, running the race and feeding your children?** (It was tricky; I didn't think I could pull it off.)

Now ask the whole class:

● **How is this like what happens in your families in real life?** (Parents have to balance a lot of responsibilities, and we can't always do a lot to help.)

Say: **Oh—I almost forgot. I have rewards for all the parents.** Pass out 3×5 cards on which you've written stress-related illnesses such as gastric ulcers, migraine headaches, nervous breakdowns and heart disease.

Ask:

● **Are these the kinds of rewards real parents earn? Explain.** (Yes, if they don't get help and support from their kids; no, my parents know how to take care of themselves.)

Say: **Let's name practical ways you can support your parents to keep them from earning the kinds of rewards I just passed out. Each suggestion you give earns you a chocolate kiss.** Record kids' responses on the left side of a sheet of newsprint.

Ask:

● **Turning the tables, what can your parents do to support you?** Record these responses on the right side of the same sheet of newsprint.

Ask:

● **What's similar about these lists? What's different?**

● **What happens if one side feels like it's doing all of the giving and none of the receiving?** (Tension and resentment build.)

Say: **Giving and receiving support needs to be a two-way street. That's what keeps families working together.**

WHAT'S YOUR ROLE?

Write the following lists on three separate sheets of posterboard.

"List A: well-organized, conscientious, serious, reliable, relates well to adults"

"List B: avoids conflict, extremely loyal to friends, goes own way, negotiator"

"List C: charming, people person, clown, easygoing, good salesperson"

Lay the lists on the floor and say: **Study each of these lists. Stand by the one that most nearly describes you.**

When kids arc in position, say: **Talk to the other people in your group and find out if there is a fairly consistent pattern to where you were born in your families (first-born or only child, middle child, last-born child).**

List A is typical of first-born or only children; list B is typical of middle children; list C typically describes last-born children. These lists are generalizations based on Dr. Kevin Leman's *The Birth Order Book.* While you may see some variation in how the kids in your group line up, chances are that many of the first-borns, middle children and last-borns will end up together.

Ask:

● **Why do you think people in your birth order develop these similar characteristics?** (First-borns shoulder lots of responsibility; middle children try to stay out of trouble and develop strong peer relationships because they don't get as much attention from parents; last-borns thrive on the attention they got for being cute when they were young.)

Say: **Birth order can have a lot to do with who we become. Let's take a look at how birth order figures in a well-known Bible story.**

Have each group look up and read Luke 15:11-32. Have the A's discuss how the behavior of the older son is like typical first-born behavior. Have the B's discuss how they think a middle son would behave in this story. Have the C's discuss why they think the youngest son made the choices he did.

Give groups about three minutes for discussion, then ask each group to report its conclusions.

Ask:

● **How big a part do you think birth order played in this story?** (A big part; it's just coincidence.)

Say: **In this story, the first-born son probably set a blazing pace of hard work and responsibility that the last-born son felt he could never match.**

Ask:

● **How much do you think your birth order has affected your personality?** (A lot; not much at all.)

Say: **Each place in the birth order has its strengths and weaknesses. But just like the sons in the story, we all make choices. We can choose to build on our strengths and overcome our weaknesses, or we can lean on our weaknesses and use them as an excuse. The one character in this story we haven't discussed is the father. Raise your hand if you agree with his open-armed forgiveness. Now raise your hand if you think he should have taken a harder line with the younger son.**

If responses fall along birth-order lines, point that fact out to the kids.

Then ask:

● **Who does the father in this story represent?** (Our heavenly Father.)

Say: **Fortunately we have a heavenly Father who is always willing to accept us, no matter where our strengths and weaknesses lie!**

ROLES RECONSIDERED

Give groups A, B and C the appropriate parts of the "Roles Reconsidered" handout (p. 29).

Say: **Read Romans 12:4-10, then apply it to the situation on your handout. Take a few minutes to decide if you like the way the situation is handled or if you'd prefer to change it. There are no right or wrong answers, and not everyone in your group has to agree.**

Allow a few minutes for groups to read and discuss, then call time and have each group present its response(s).

Ask:

● **Did you feel that the behavior described in the handout is typical of something you might do? Explain.** (Yes, I'm a lot like that; no, I might think like that, but I'd never do it.)

● **How are your personal characteristics an asset to your family?** (I keep everyone cheerful; I help resolve conflicts; I can be counted on to get things done.)

● **How are they a possible detriment?** (Sometimes I blow off responsibility; I let my own priorities get in the way; I tend to be critical.)

Say: **Tell the other members of your group one thing you'll do this week to show consideration and understanding to someone in your family.**

☐ OPTION 1: FAMILY ASSETS

Form a circle. If you have more than a dozen kids in your group, form two circles. Distribute paper plates and markers. Have kids write their names on their plates and set the plates

COMMITMENT
(5 to 10 minutes)

CLOSING
(up to 5 minutes)

on the floor in front of them.

Say: **Everyone rotate one position to the left. Write on the plate in front of you how that person is an asset to his or her family. We'll keep rotating and writing until you come back to your own plate.**

When the kids have gone clear around the circle, toss the plates in a pile in the center of the circle. Then join hands and close in prayer: **Thank you, Lord, for the gifts and strengths you've given each person. Help us use those gifts and strengths to build strong, caring families. In Jesus' name, amen.**

Encourage teenagers to take their plates home.

☐ OPTION 2: SURPRISED!

Have kids form pairs.

Say: **Tell your partner one surprising thing you've learned about yourself today and how you can use that information to strengthen yourself and your family. Then close by saying a sentence prayer for your partner and his or her family.**

If You Still Have Time . . .

Responsibility Cards—Distribute 3×5 cards and pencils. Have kids list on their cards tasks and responsibilities they have in their families. Gather the cards, then scramble and redistribute them. Have kids each take turns reading the card they're holding and guess whose card it is. Discuss what is a reasonable responsibility level for teenagers at home.

Crisis Zone—Have kids each tell about a time they were preoccupied with their own agenda and unintentionally caused a minicrisis in their family.

Roles Reconsidered

Photocopy and cut apart the following three sections and give them to the appropriate groups.

GROUP A

Read Romans 12:4-10, then discuss the situation below.

You and your younger brother have the responsibility of cleaning and decorating the house for a surprise 25th anniversary party for your parents. You have done the major part of the cleaning while your brother has been entertaining himself with video games in the basement.

Your brother has great artistic flair, and you don't have much of an idea of how to decorate. But you're disgusted with your brother's lack of responsibility so you put up a few streamers, then go to the basement and chew your brother out for leaving everything up to you.

GROUP B

Read Romans 12:4-10, then discuss the situation below.

One of your friends has taped 20 episodes of *Star Trek* for a Trekathon weekend at his or her house. You're looking forward to a great weekend with your friends. But your younger brother's soccer team unexpectedly makes the playoffs, and the semifinals are the night of the Trekathon. You tell your mom, "I've spent half my life watching Eric play soccer. Besides, I don't think it's fair to let my friends down. We've been planning this for a long time."

GROUP C

Read Romans 12:4-10, then discuss the situation below.

You're sitting through your older sister's piano recital, and you're bored out of your mind. All the young kids are playing first, and it will be at least 45 minutes until your sister gets her shot at Beethoven's "Moonlight Sonata." Your mom reaches for something in her purse, and you spot her small mirror. When you slip the mirror out of her purse, the light hits it and reflects off the bald head of a man sitting three rows in front of you. You begin bouncing the light all over the room and then back to the bald head. A few people notice and begin to chuckle. You're very glad you've found something to relieve your boredom and entertain the people around you.

LESSON 3

THE NUCLEAR FAMILY

For some teenagers, conflict starts the moment their feet hit the floor in the morning and doesn't let up until they fall back into bed at night. We could call the family where this happens a "nuclear" family, not meaning immediate or birth family, but rather the family whose house is a war zone.

Some family conflict is inevitable, but there's no reason for teenagers to live in constant conflict. Use this lesson to help your students gain skills to deal with conflict in positive, Christlike ways.

LESSON AIM

To help senior highers learn how to resolve conflict in positive, Christlike ways.

OBJECTIVES

Students will
- experience the futility of yelling matches,
- learn that what they say isn't necessarily what people hear,
- identify typical areas of conflict,
- make a clear plan for conflict resolution and
- plan ways to defuse future conflicts.

BIBLE BASIS

MATTHEW 18:15-16
LUKE 10:38-42

Look up the following scriptures. Then read the background paragraphs to see how the passages relate to your senior highers.

In **Matthew 18:15-16**, Jesus gives simple yet profound advice for settling conflicts: "If your brother sins against you, go and show him his fault."

Jesus does not call us to be doormats or members of the Milquetoast family. Nor does he call us to swallow our anger and calmly persuade ourselves that conflict doesn't exist.

Teenagers need to understand that they can resolve knotty family issues without giving in or blowing their tops. "Go and show him his fault" tells us that Jesus expects calm but direct confrontation. This is definitely not a cowardly approach! And it's not something that can be pulled off without forethought, an understanding of what makes the other guy tick and a sincere desire to see both sides of the issue.

Luke 10:38-42 tells the story of Mary and Martha. Martha is frantic with all the preparation required to have Jesus and his followers as guests in her home. Meanwhile, Mary sits calmly at Jesus' feet, drinking in his teaching, unconcerned about everything else that needs to be done. Martha petitions Jesus to send Mary to the kitchen. Jesus patiently replies that "Mary has chosen what is better." Jesus knew that mealtimes would come and go, but he would only be present to teach his followers for a few short months.

In some families the term "brotherly love" seems like an oxymoron—a phrase that contradicts itself. Differing priorities, values, schedules and needs cause conflict between siblings and parents. For kids, this is the training ground where they learn conflict resolution patterns that will probably stay with them most of their lives. Kids need to learn that conflicts can be resolved peacefully so that everybody wins.

THIS LESSON AT A GLANCE

Section	Minutes	What Students Will Do	Supplies
Opener (Option 1) (Option 2)	5 to 10	**Yellathon**—Yell messages at one another. **Where's Mine?**—Solve a situation where there aren't enough treats for everyone.	Whistle Candy bars
Action and Reflection	10 to 15	**Is That What I Said?**—Communicate to partners how to draw a picture.	"Draw This" handouts (p. 37), pencils, paper
Bible Application	15 to 20	**Nuclear Conflict**—Compare the conflict between Mary and Martha to typical conflicts in their families.	Bibles, "War Zone" handouts (p. 38), pencils
Commitment	5 to 10	**Be It Resolved**—Choose conflict resolution strategies.	Bible, newsprint, marker
Closing (Option 1) (Option 2)	up to 5	**Potholes and Pitfalls**—Identify future conflicts and how to defuse them. **Have It Your Way**—Pledge to resolve conflicts in Christlike ways.	

The Lesson

☐ OPTION 1: YELLATHON

Form two groups. Call the first group of kids into a huddle and whisper their instructions. On your signal they're to yell the words of "Take Me Out to the Ballgame" at the other group as loudly as they can. Explain that they are to yell the words, not sing them.

Call the second group of kids into a huddle and whisper that on your signal they're each to yell a pizza order at the other group as loudly as possible. Have them include what kind and how many pizzas they want and their names and telephone numbers.

Since this activity produces lots of noise, consider taking kids to a place in the church where the noise won't bother other classes.

Have groups face each other. Blow the whistle to begin the yelling match. Allow the yelling to go on for 15 to 20 seconds, then blow the whistle again to halt it.

Congratulate kids on the decibel level they were able to produce.

Then ask:

● **Who can tell me what the other group was yelling?** Most kids will have little or no knowledge of what they heard.

● **How is this like what sometimes happens in families?** (Once we start yelling at each other, we don't have any idea of what the other guy is saying.)

● **Do conflicts ever get settled this way? Explain.** (Yes, sometimes the person who yells the loudest wins; no, both people just go away mad.)

● **What are other unproductive techniques for settling conflicts?** (Slamming doors; going away mad; throwing things; making threats.)

● **Do you think most conflicts can be resolved so that everyone feels like a winner? Explain.** (No, that's never happened to me; yes, you can work things out.)

Say: **Today we're going to look at typical conflicts that come up in every family and discover new approaches to conflict resolution that will help turn down the decibel level of the yelling matches at your house.**

☐ OPTION 2: WHERE'S MINE?

Form groups of four or five. Toss each group one fewer candy bar than there are members in the group.

Say: **Treats are on the house today. Go ahead and "sweeten up" as you share with your group members one typical conflict that happens in your family.**

If kids point out that they didn't receive enough candy bars, ignore them. Join one of the groups and tell about a typical conflict that came up when you were a teenager. After groups have shared, call everyone together and say: **I set you up for a conflict by not giving you enough candy bars for your entire group.**

Ask:

● **How did you handle that conflict?** (Someone shared half of his or her candy bar with the person who didn't get one; we all gave the person who didn't get one a bite.)

● **Suppose that same conflict had happened at your house. Would you have handled it the same way you did here? Explain.** (Yes, we all would have shared part of our candy bars; no, I probably would have said, "You've eaten most of the candy bars, so this one is mine.")

● **Do you handle conflicts in your family the same way you handle conflicts with your friends? Explain.** (No, I'm careful with my friends, but I really let my temper fly at home; yes, we all work hard at coming up with peaceful solutions at home.)

Say: **Conflicts are a natural part of family life. How we choose to handle those conflicts has a lot to do with the kind of atmosphere we have at home. Today we're going to discover simple, effective ways to approach conflict resolution.**

IS THAT WHAT I SAID?

Have kids form pairs and sit back to back on the floor, with plenty of space between each pair. Give one partner a copy of the "Draw This" handout (p. 37); give the other partner a pencil and a sheet of paper.

Say: **Those of you who have the "Draw This" handout are to give your partners verbal instructions that will help them reproduce on their papers the picture you're look-ing at. You have two minutes to create your master-pieces. Go!**

Call time after two minutes and have partners compare the picture they created to the "Draw This" handout. Give a hearty round of applause to each of the artists.

Then ask:

● **What was so difficult about this activity?** (It was hard to tell exactly what I was supposed to draw; it was difficult to give clear directions.)

● **What does this show you about communication?** (It's not easy to say what you mean; people can take the things you say in different ways.)

● **How is this lack of clear communication like what sometimes happens in families?** (People don't always un-derstand things the way you mean them.)

Say: **When conflict is in the air and emotions are run-ning high, we really need to listen between the lines. I'll**

ACTION AND REFLECTION
(10 to 15 minutes)

give you some examples. You listen between the lines and tell me what I might really be saying.

● **Just leave me alone.** (I'm having a really bad day.)

● **You idiot!** (I'm totally frustrated, and I'm turning my frustration on you.)

● **I don't have to listen to this.** (It would be more constructive to talk about this another time.)

● **You always do this to me!** (This is a problem we've had before, and we need to find a solution.)

● **I can't believe how stupid I am.** (I'm disappointed with myself, and I don't know how anyone could like me.)

Say: **Listening between the lines is one of the skills that will help us learn how to work through conflicts. Now let's listen between the lines of a very famous argument between sisters.**

BIBLE APPLICATION

(15 to 20 minutes)

NUCLEAR CONFLICT

Have kids look up Luke 10:38-42. Ask a volunteer to read the passage aloud.

Then ask:

● **Whose side are you on in this conflict?** (Martha's—I don't think she should have had to do all the work; Mary's—she knew what was most important.)

● **How do you feel about the answer Jesus gave?** (He showed that he cared for Martha by the way he said her name; I don't understand why he didn't make Mary help.)

● **Is asking someone you respect to be a mediator a legitimate way to settle a conflict?** (Yes, because you get an objective opinion; no, it's like telling on someone.)

Say: **Mary and Martha's home was suddenly full of visitors—important visitors. That's enough to add stress to any family! Let's find out what kinds of situations can turn your house into a war zone.**

Distribute the "War Zone" handouts (p. 38) and pencils. Give kids a couple of minutes to rate their top five conflict points. Then tally the number of kids who checked each item to discover the top hot spots for your youth group.

Say: **Now that we know what your hot spots are, let's figure out what to do about them. Find a partner and share your answers to these questions.**

● **Of the hot spots you checked, which can you take personal responsibility for?**

● **What action can you take to keep these conflicts from recurring?**

● **How do you feel about the way your parents handle these conflicts? What do you wish they'd do differently?**

Say: **Let's turn our attention to some techniques you can use to resolve these conflicts. Our first one comes from Jesus himself.**

BE IT RESOLVED

Have a volunteer read aloud Matthew 18:15-16. Then ask:

● **What do you think about this advice from Jesus?** (You have to be brave to do that; most people don't want to hear what they've done wrong; you need to be careful how you approach the person.)

Say: **When you're trying to settle a conflict, timing and attitude are everything. Here are some simple guidelines.** Write these points on a sheet of newsprint:

● Take time out.
● Put yourself in the other person's shoes.
● Listen.
● Learn to say, "I'm sorry."

Say: **Now let's go through these points, and you tell me why they're important.**

Ask:

● **What's the point of taking a timeout?** (You get perspective on the situation; you get rid of the adrenaline rush and think more clearly; if you keep on talking when you're mad, you end up saying things you don't really mean.)

● **Why is it important to put yourself in the other person's shoes?** (Because every story has two sides; you need to realize how your actions affect other people.)

● **How can you let people know you're really listening?** (By looking them in the eye and nodding your head; by rephrasing what they say and asking if that's correct.)

● **Why is listening so important?** (It shows respect for the other person's point of view; if you listen to others, they'll be more inclined to listen to you.)

● **What are the hardest words to say in any language?** (I'm sorry.)

● **Why is saying them so important?** (Because it's healthy to accept responsibility for our mistakes; because it opens the way toward resolution and healing.)

Say: **One last thing—it's important to realize that you can't change anyone else's behavior. You can only change your own behavior and your own reactions. These aren't simple solutions that will suddenly make everything okay in your lives. But they're important tools you can use to resolve conflict in a Christlike way.**

Form pairs. Have kids take turns completing the following sentence about their partners: "You'll be good at resolving conflict because . . . " Encourage kids to say positive reasons their partners can succeed such as "You are sensitive to others" or "You know how to communicate well."

☐ OPTION 1: POTHOLES AND PITFALLS

Say: **Tell your partner about one conflict you'll probably face soon. It may be something from the "War Zone" handout, or it may be one of those potholes and pitfalls**

COMMITMENT
(5 to 10 minutes)

CLOSING
(up to 5 minutes)

that are part of family life. Then discuss together a plan of action for defusing or resolving that conflict.

Allow a few minutes for partners to share. Then have partners pray for each other's conflicts and their ability to resolve them.

☐ OPTION 2: HAVE IT YOUR WAY

Have students form a circle. Ask:

● **What did you feel like doing or saying the last time you were really mad at somebody?** (I wanted to smack them; I wished I could have sent them to Siberia; I wanted to tell them off.)

Say: **Sometimes you may think it would feel really good just to clobber the people you butt heads with. But Jesus calls us to do things his way. Let's bow our heads and close with sentence prayers committing ourselves to doing things the Christlike way and asking God for the strength to do that.**

If You Still Have Time . . .

Take Two—Form groups of no more than five. Have each group dream up and role play a conflict situation. Have the other groups suggest how to resolve each conflict based on the techniques they learned in today's lesson.

From the Screen—Discuss how conflict is handled in kids' favorite TV shows. Compare those examples to Jesus' teaching.

DRAW THIS

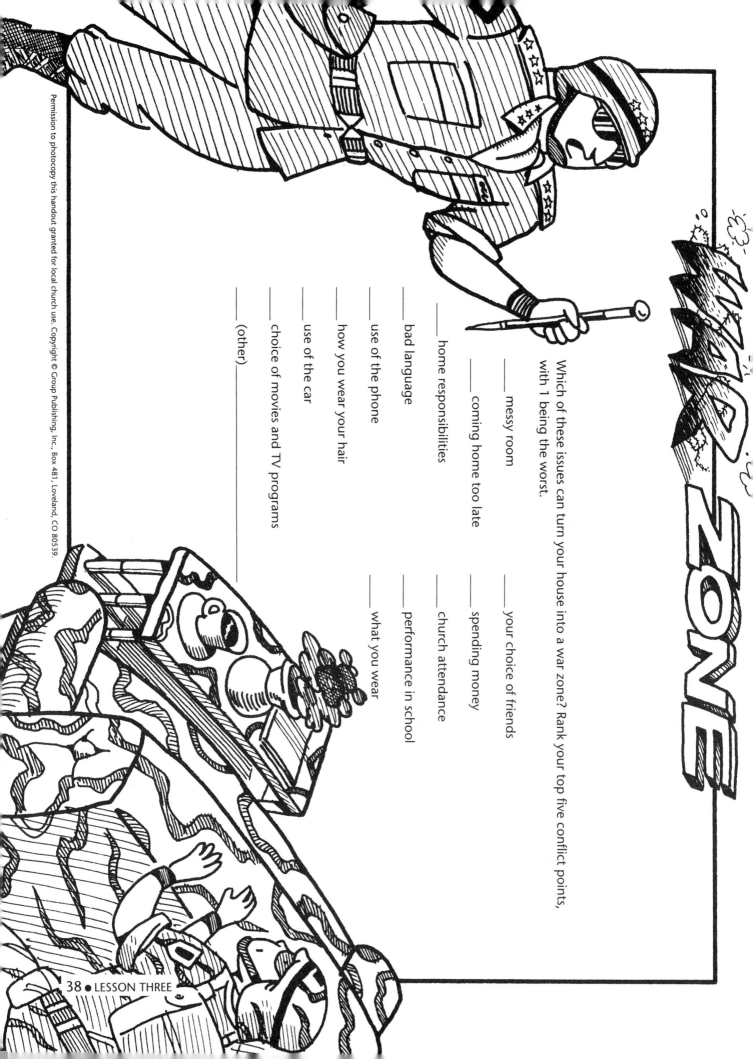

WAR ZONE

Which of these issues can turn your house into a war zone? Rank your top five conflict points, with 1 being the worst.

_____ messy room

_____ coming home too late

_____ your choice of friends

_____ spending money

_____ church attendance

_____ performance in school

_____ what you wear

_____ home responsibilities

_____ bad language

_____ use of the phone

_____ how you wear your hair

_____ use of the car

_____ choice of movies and TV programs

_____ (other) _____

YOUR FUTURE FAMILY

LESSON 4

Senior highers are just a few short years from making marriage and career decisions that will have a huge impact on the rest of their lives. This lesson will help kids see that the positive steps they take in relating to their present families will build a strong foundation for their families of the future.

To help senior highers think through their goals and dreams for their future families.

LESSON AIM

Students will
- **realize how soon they'll be making life-changing decisions about family and career,**
- **create sculptures that express who they are,**
- **compare their present families to how they envision their future families,**
- **make commitments to affirm members of their families and**
- **affirm each other's potential for building strong relationships.**

OBJECTIVES

Look up the following scriptures. Then read the background paragraphs to see how the passages relate to your senior highers.

Jeremiah 29:11-13 describes Jeremiah's assurance that the bad times won't last forever.

This passage is one of the Bible's most reassuring promises. Speaking to the Israelites in exile, Jeremiah assured God's people that the time would come when God would restore their land and give them a hope and a future.

Many of today's teenagers face the future with a great deal of trepidation. They may cover it with a bold front, but in their moments of honesty they'll confess to apprehensive

BIBLE BASIS
JEREMIAH 29:11-13
MATTHEW 7:24-27

feelings. Life tends to run on automatic pilot until the end of high school, then suddenly kids have to take the controls. What a great thing to tell teenagers that they're not alone—that God has a hope and a future for those who trust their lives to him.

In **Matthew 7:24-27**, Jesus contrasts the solid foundation of his teaching to the shifting sands of worldly wisdom and personal opinion.

Human beings can be pretty cocky creatures. We like to figure things out for ourselves. Swallowing authority just doesn't sit well. Jesus commends those who hear his words and put them into practice, saying that those people will stand against winds of adversity.

An astonishing number of Christian kids feel that sexual experimentation before marriage is okay. Christian values seem quaint and unattainable in the face of what society deems "normal." In the face of intense sexual pressure and temptation, Christian kids need to see that the only way to stand strong is to hear Jesus' words and put them into practice.

THIS LESSON AT A GLANCE

Section	Minutes	What Students Will Do	Supplies
Opener (Option 1)	5 to 10	**Well-Aged**—Retouch photographs to make them look older.	Photocopies of group members' photos, colored pencils
(Option 2)		**Not Me!**—Tell embarrassing things their parents have done that they would never repeat.	
Action and Reflection	10 to 15	**Unfinished**—Create sculptures that represent who they are.	Modeling clay
Bible Application	15 to 20	**Solid Ground**—Compare the solid ground of biblical teaching about marriage to the shifting sands of society's views.	Newsprint, Bibles, marker, slips of paper, pencils, "What's Your Family Type?" envelopes from the Family Types activity in Lesson 1
Commitment	5 to 10	**Investing for the Future**—Affirm their present family members.	Markers, "Family Care Card" handouts (p. 45)
Closing (Option 1)	up to 5	**Fabulous Futures**—Tell each other why God has a great future planned for them.	Bibles
(Option 2)		**Things Change**—Describe how their family relationships have changed.	Bible

The Lesson

☐ OPTION 1: WELL-AGED

Take Polaroid head shots of kids as they arrive. Photocopy the pictures, enlarging them if possible. Or prepare enlarged, photocopied photos of kids before the meeting.

Set out colored pencils and give each student a photocopied picture of someone else. Challenge kids to age their person 20 or 30 years. Allow a couple of minutes for artistic sabotage, then bring everyone together to display the "retouched" portraits.

Ask:

● **How did it feel to "age" the person whose picture you had?** (It was fun; I kept wondering what was happening to my picture.)

● **How did it feel to see yourself aged 20 or 30 years?** (It's hilarious; I can't believe I'm ever going to be that old.)

● **Do you ever think about getting old?** (No, I just think about getting through the next week; it's hard to imagine myself as a person in my 30s or 40s.)

● **One trait that's typical of teenagers is a feeling of immortality—like life will go on and on. Is that how you feel? Explain.** (Yes, I never really think very far ahead; no, since my friend died, I understand how fragile life is.)

● **How secure do you feel about your post-high school plans?** (I know just what I want to do; I haven't made up my mind about college or a job.)

Say: **Life has a way of sneaking up on you. One day you're in high school, and the next thing you know you look like this.** *(Gesture toward the portraits.)* **Today we're going to consider a topic that you may never have given much thought to—your future family.**

☐ OPTION 2: NOT ME!

Ask:

● **What's something that your parents do that totally embarrasses you? something that you swear you'll never do to your kids?** Spark the discussion by sharing an anecdote from your own teenage years.

Say: **The interesting thing is that when you do get to be parents, chances are you'll do things a lot like your parents did them.**

Ask:

● **Can you see yourself 15 or 20 years in the future saying, "What I just said sounded just like my dad"? Why or why not?** (No way would I ever sound like my parents; yes, because they're the example of parenting that I know best.)

OPENER
(5 to 10 minutes)

● **How many years on average do you think it'll be until the majority of this group is married?** (Six to 10 years; I'm never getting married!)

● **How many years do you think it will be until most of you have children?** (Never! Ten to 12 years.)

Say: **Life has this interesting way of accelerating. It seems like you'll never get to high school, you'll never get your driver's license—then boom! You graduate, you go to college or get a job, and the next thing you know you're married and changing diapers. Sounds horrible, doesn't it? Today we're going to talk about your future family and see how the family relationships you're building right now can influence your family of the future.**

UNFINISHED

Form a circle. If you have more than a dozen kids in your group, form two circles. Give each student a hunk of modeling clay.

Say: **Form this clay into a sculpture that expresses something about who you are. I'll give you three minutes.**

Let kids begin their sculptures but stop them after about a minute. Say: **That's all the time we have; who's ready to tell us about your sculpture?**

If kids protest that they didn't have the promised amount of time to finish their sculptures, ignore them and ask:

● **How are your unfinished sculptures like the people you are right now?** (We're still learning and growing; our personalities and skills are still developing.)

● **Suppose I take two of these unfinished sculptures and join them together. Do you think it would create a thing of beauty? Explain.** (No, because they weren't created to be joined together; no, because neither one of them is really complete; it would keep both of the sculptures from reaching their potential.)

● **How would putting two unfinished sculptures together be like a couple getting married right out of high school?** (It would be hard for them to reach their potential; it would be a wobbly sculpture and a wobbly marriage.)

Say: **Go ahead and finish your sculpture. This time I promise to give you the time you need. Make your sculpture represent the kind of person you'd like to become before you join another person in marriage.**

Allow two or three minutes for kids to finish their sculptures. Then go around the group allowing each person to tell about his or her sculpture.

After everyone has shared, say: **I believe you can meet those goals, especially if you build your lives on Christ.**

ACTION AND REFLECTION
(10 to 15 minutes)

SOLID GROUND

Put up two large sheets of newsprint. Have kids turn to Matthew 7:24-27. Ask a volunteer to read it aloud. Then label one sheet of newsprint "solid rock"; label the other sheet of newsprint "shifting sand."

Say: **Let's compare the solid rock of biblical teaching about marriage with the shifting sands of society's views.**

Print the following Bible references on slips of paper: Matthew 5:27; Matthew 15:17-20; Matthew 19:4-9; 1 Corinthians 6:9-10; 1 Corinthians 6:18-20; 2 Corinthians 6:14; Ephesians 5:22-28; Ephesians 6:1-4.

Hand out the slips. Have students read, then paraphrase their verses. Jot their paraphrases on the "solid rock" newsprint, then invite the class to state society's view of the issue. Jot those responses on the "shifting sand" newsprint.

Then point to the "solid rock" sheet and ask:

● **What's difficult about doing things God's way?** (It's hard because it feels like we're the only few people in the world who are trying to hold to those standards.)

● **What are the risks of doing things the world's way?** (You risk getting sexually transmitted diseases; you slowly destroy yourself.)

● **What are the advantages of doing things God's way?** (It's harder, but it gives you a lot better chance of succeeding; God takes care of people who honor him.)

Distribute pencils and the envelopes containing the "What's Your Family Type?" handout kids completed in the Family Types activity in Lesson 1. Give blank handouts to any kids who missed that lesson.

Say: **In Lesson 1 you rated your family type in several categories. Then you rated where you personally fit in each category. Now, keeping in mind the biblical principles we just listed, mark with an arrow where you'd like your future family to fit.**

Allow a minute or so for kids to mark their papers. Then say: **Now here's an even more interesting challenge. Turn your paper over and write 10 characteristics you'd look for in a future husband or wife.**

Call time after about two minutes and ask volunteers to name the characteristics they listed. Have the class vote on the three most important characteristics. Encourage kids to put their handouts back in their envelopes and to keep them for future reference.

Say: **The good relationships and positive habits you establish now will form a solid foundation for the family you may have in the future.**

INVESTING FOR THE FUTURE

Distribute a marker and the "Family Care Card" handout (p. 45) to each student.

Say: **Many of us have a tendency to let our family mem-**

bers know when they goof up, but we're not as faithful about expressing our appreciation for the things they do right. Take time right now to write one of the care cards for someone in your family.

Give kids a couple of minutes to write. Then say: **Now pair up and tell your partner who you wrote your note to, where you're going to put it, and what you think that person's reaction will be when he or she reads it.**

Have teenagers each write a "Family Care Card" for their partner, affirming a positive quality they've seen in him or her during the past few weeks. For example, kids might write "You've been a great partner!" or "You really know how to express your ideas."

CLOSING
(up to 5 minutes)

☐ OPTION 1: FABULOUS FUTURES

Have each pair join another pair to form groups of four. Have groups look up and read Jeremiah 29:11-13.

Then say: **Tell the person sitting across from you why you think God has great plans for his or her future. Begin with the person who's wearing the most red.**

Have groups close with prayer, asking God to help them build the best family relationships possible, both now and in the future.

☐ OPTION 2: THINGS CHANGE

Have each pair join another pair to form groups of four. Ask each person to share how his or her family relationship has changed since beginning this study. Then bring everyone together in a circle and read aloud Jeremiah 29:11-13.

Say: **Our families are really the proving ground where we develop as people. When we work to make our family relationships the best they can be, we can be sure that we have hope and a future.**

Have groups each close with prayer asking God to help them keep on working to build strong, healthy relationships in their families.

If You Still Have Time . . .

Whose Future?—Distribute paper and pencils. Have kids each write anonymous predictions about themselves 30 years from now. Collect and redistribute the papers. Have kids read the predictions they're holding and guess whose they are.

Course Reflection—Form a circle. Ask students to reflect on the past four lessons. Have them take turns completing the following sentences:
- Something I learned in this course is . . .
- If I could tell my friends about this course, I'd say . . .
- Something I'll do differently because of this course is . . .

FAMILY Care Card

YOU'RE THE GREATEST!

THANKS FOR BEING THERE.

YOU'RE NICE TO HAVE AROUND.

THREE CHEERS FOR YOU!

BONUS IDEAS

Bonus Scriptures—The lessons focus on a select few scripture passages, but if you'd like to incorporate more Bible readings into the lesson, here are our suggestions:
- Ruth 1:16-17 (Ruth says she'll stay with Naomi.)
- Psalm 127 (The psalmist describes children as a gift from God.)
- Proverbs 23:22 (Listen to your father and don't forget your mother.)
- Jeremiah 32:39 (People want to worship God for the sake of their children.)
- Acts 16:25-34 (Paul and Silas tell a jailer's family about Jesus.)

Family Feuds—Have kids dramatize famous family feuds from the book of Genesis: Cain and Abel, Jacob and Esau, and Joseph and his brothers. Suggest that kids create melodramas with a witty moral. Get permission to raid the Christmas costume closet for Bible costumes or bring a fine selection of old bathrobes and towels.

Letters From the Past—Early in this study, have a letter-writing night in which kids write to their oldest living relatives asking for interesting bits of family history. Tell kids to enclose stamped, self-addressed envelopes for their relatives' convenience.

At the end of the study, plan a special Nostalgia Night ice cream social where kids make homemade ice cream (preferably with a hand-crank ice cream maker) and read aloud the replies they received. This is a really fascinating way to get kids in touch with their family histories!

Take My Advice—Set up a panel discussion with a pastor, a professional marriage counselor and a social worker. Have each panel member tell about his or her work in helping troubled families. Then open the session for questions from kids.

The Dating Game—Borrow your teenagers' parents for a special edition of *The Newlywed Game*. With the mothers out of the room, ask the fathers these questions:
- **When did you meet your spouse?**
- **Where did you go on your first date?**
- **What was the first gift you received from her?**
- **What day of the week did you get married?**
- **Were there any glitches at your wedding? Explain.**
- **Where did you go for your honeymoon?**

● **How many years until (or since) your 25th anniversary?**

Then bring in the mothers and ask them the same questions. Give a dinner gift certificate to the couple with the most matching answers.

Table Talk—Help kids plan and prepare a special night for giving their parents their "just desserts." Have kids meet the night before to do the cooking and decorating. Have kids make place cards with affirming messages such as "This spot is reserved for Molly's marvelous mom." Have parents and kids work through the desserts and the "Table Talk" handout (p. 20). End the evening with a standing ovation for the parents.

That Was Then, This Is Now—Make this a fun event for parents and teenagers based on the "That Was Then, This Is Now" handout (p. 48). For the event, have kids dress as their parents dressed when they were teenagers; have parents dress like today's teenagers.

When We Were Five—Have a party with an early childhood theme. Have kids dress as they did when they were five years old. Invite them to bring favorite photos, toys and memorabilia they've saved. Play children's party games such as Pin the Tail on the Donkey, London Bridge and Blind Man's Bluff. Serve red Kool-Aid, cupcakes and lollipops. At some point in the party, have kids tell their favorite childhood memories, as well as their worst childhood memories. Note: Be sensitive to kids who may have come from abusive family backgrounds.

Families Away—Plan an overnight retreat or lock-in with a family theme. Have kids each bring a baby picture as their admission. Display the pictures and have kids guess who's who. Play a few rounds of *Family Feud* as a warm-up. Then launch into a marathon video session of old family shows such as *The Adventures of Ozzie and Harriet* or *Father Knows Best*. At each "intermission" discuss how the values in the show compare to biblical values and to values portrayed in TV shows today. After the video session, give kids quiet time to write letters to their parents and siblings expressing how they feel about them.

Close the retreat by having kids prepare a gourmet breakfast for their youth group "family."

That Was Then, This Is Now

PARENT	TEENAGER
Jobs I had as a teenager:	Jobs I have as a teenager:
My #1 worry as a teenager:	My #1 worry as a teenager:
The really "in" thing to wear was:	The really "in" thing to wear is:
The one thing I really wanted was:	The one thing I really want is:
Big social issues during my teenage years were:	Big social issues during my teenage years are:
My favorite thing about church was:	My favorite thing about church is:
My favorite music was:	My favorite music is:
My goal for my life was:	My goal for my life is: